Special thanks to: The British Tourist Authority for use of the photograph of Buckingham Palace on page 6. The White House Photo Office for use of the photograph of the White House on page 9. The Canadian Consulate General for use of the photographs of the Innuit hunter and tent on page 15, and snowbound house on page 27.

Library of Congress Cataloging in Publication Data
Morris, Ann, Houses and homes / by Ann Morris ; photographs by Ken Heyman.
    p.   cm. Summary: A simple discussion of different kinds of houses and what makes them homes. ISBN 0-688-10168-2.
— ISBN 0-688-10169-0 (lib. bdg.)   1. Housing—Juvenile literature.   2. Dwellings—Juvenile literature.   [1. Dwellings.]
I. Heyman, Ken, ill.   II. Title.   HD7287.M65 1992   363.5—dc20 92-1365 CIP AC

ANN MORRIS

◆◆

HOUSES AND HOMES

PHOTOGRAPHS BY
KEN HEYMAN

LOTHROP, LEE & SHEPARD BOOKS

NEW YORK

The world is full of houses ...

5

big houses

little houses

bright houses

white houses

houses that move

and houses that stay

in a row

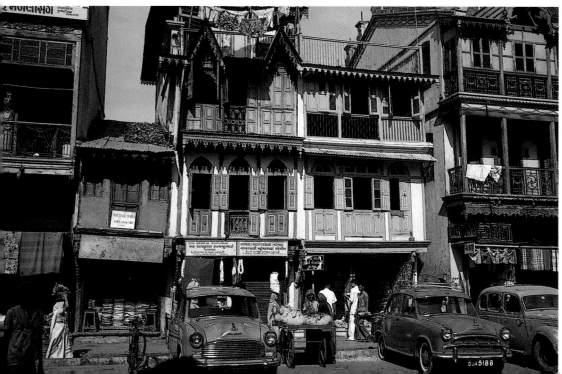

or all alone

filled with families

just right for one.

Build your house with what is handy … wood

or stone

or straw

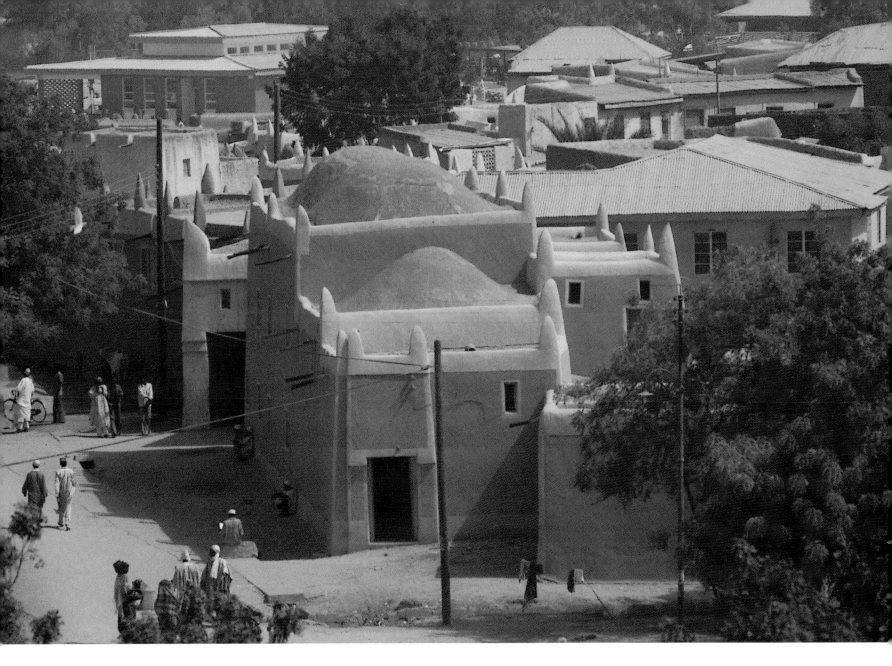

or mud

or almost anything at all.

Weave it

nail it

23

tie it with rope.

Build it on stilts!

Let in the air to keep it cool.

Fill in the cracks to keep it warm.

Fill it with love

and make it a home.

INDEX

15 CANADA: While they travel in search of game, Innuit hunters live in one-man tents such as this one, made of warm, waterproof animal hide.

16 UNITED STATES: This Navajo hogan is made of wood and earth. No nails are used. The logs are cut to fit together snugly.

17 RUSSIA: The dense forests that cover the Russian countryside provide plenty of lumber for wooden houses.

17 GUATEMALA: Walls made of narrow stakes tied together let air in to cool this house in hot weather, but keep the rain out.

18 ITALY: Stone houses last for hundreds of years. Many generations of the same family may have grown up in this farmhouse.

19 PERU: The land here is covered with rocks, which are used to build sturdy stone houses.

20 PAPUA NEW GUINEA: The men of this village are weaving palm fronds into large mats to make the walls and floor for a new house. The roof will be thatched with bound straw.

21 NIGERIA: These town houses are made of mud bricks and plastered with mud to seal the cracks. The walls are very thick to keep out the hot sun and burning desert wind.

22 KENYA: This Samburu chief naps outside his house, which is made of sticks, rags, vines, paper, cardboard, pots, mud, and other materials found near his village.

23 BALI: These men are weaving a mat for a floor or wall from fronds that grow throughout their island home.

24 KENYA: In this village, house building is a community activity. Women work as a team to lash the frame of a new home together with rope and vines.

25 THAILAND: These houses are built on stilts to keep them above water at high tide. Here canals are used as streets.

26 BALI: The walls of this tropical home are made from bamboo screens that can be rolled up to let in breezes or tied down to keep out the sun or rain.

27 CANADA: The tall stovepipe on this log cabin sticks up high so that it will not be covered by snow.

28 KENYA: A loving father takes care of his children in front of their round home.

29 UNITED STATES: The front porch of this house in Appalachia is a favorite gathering place for this family.

Where in the world were these photographs taken?

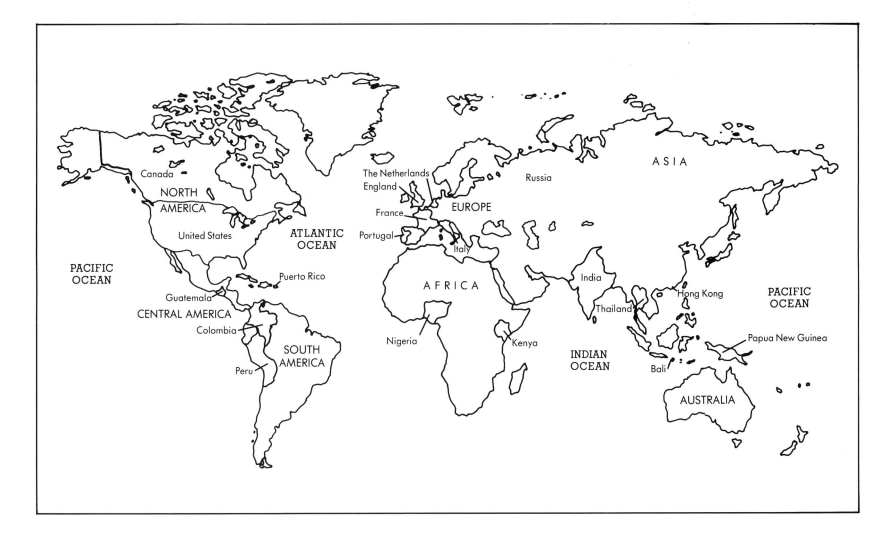